QUILTS

From Colonial to Contemporary

Contributing Writer
Lacy Folmar Bullard

PUBLICATIONS INTERNATIONAL, LTD.

Louis Weber, C.E.O.
Publications International, Ltd.
7373 North Cicero Ave.
Lincolnwood, IL 60646

Permission is never granted for commercial purposes.

Manufactured in U.S.A.

8 7 6 5 4 3 2 1

ISBN 1-56173-299-0

Front cover:
Pat Gaska/Siede Preis Photography (top); **Appalachian Fireside Quilts/Siede Preis Photography** (right); **Rose Sanders/Siede Preis Photography** (bottom); **Geneva Watts/Siede Preis Photography** (left); **Esther Hershberger/Siede Preis Photography** (center).

Back cover:
Esther Hershberger/Siede Preis Photography

Bernice P. Bishop Museum: 48, 49; **Michael Cummings/Siede Preis Photography:** 83; **Helen Giddens/Siede Preis Photography:** 93; **Steve Gottlieb/FPG International:** 96; **Esther Hershberger/Siede Preis Photography:** title page, table of contents; **Photography Courtesy of The Kentucky Quilt Project, Inc.:** 7, 8, 23, 33, 44, 47, 50; **Merrill Mason/Eric Landsberg Photography:** 79, 88, 89; **Collection of Eleanor and Rowland Miller/Photograph Courtesy of Shelly Zegart:** 19; **Judith Montaño/Siede Preis Photography:** 82; **Clare M. Murray/Siede Preis Photography:** 90, 91; **Ruth M. Norton/Siede Preis Photography:** 78; **Robert Rathe/FPG International:** 95; **Joan M. Rigal/Siede Preis Photography:** 85; **Jane Sassaman:** 92; **Lois Tornquist Smith/Siede Preis Photography:** 86; **Spencer Museum of Art:** 4, 5, 18, 36, 52, 72, 73, 74, 75; **Collection of Shelly Zegart:** 14, 17, 20, 30, 38, 43, 51, 54, 57, 58, 59, 61, 64, 65, 68, 69, 70, 71, 77, 80 (bottom), 84; **Photography Courtesy of Shelly Zegart:** 6, 9, 10, 11, 12, 13, 15, 16, 21, 22, 24, 25, 26, 27, 28, 29, 31, 32, 34, 35, 37, 39, 40, 41, 42, 45, 46, 53, 55, 56, 60, 62, 63, 66, 67, 76, 80 (top), 81, 87, 94.

Contributing Writer Lacy Folmar Bullard is a writer, consultant, and editor with a special interest in quilts. She wrote *Chintz Quilts: Unfading Glory* with Betty Jo Shiell and has been a contributing writer to *Quilter's Digest*. Her time is divided between Tallahassee, Florida, and Sugarcamp Farm, in the North Carolina mountains near Asheville.

Consultant Virginia Gunn is an associate professor at the University of Akron where she teaches courses in the history of design, textile arts, and textile conservation. She is curator of the University's historic costume and textile collections and serves as a consultant for regional historical agencies. Virginia is also president of the board of directors of the American Quilt Study Group.

Contents

Introduction

Imagination, dreams, and the many hundreds of hours of skilled work required to make thousands of tiny, perfect stitches have made American quilts much more than serviceable, homemade bed covers.

Left: Sage Bud or Goose Tracks, made of pieced blocks, is set together with diagonal sashing and nine-patch crossings and combined with an appliqué border on only two sides. The quilt was probably made sometime between 1840 and 1875. Above: Floral is a boldly appliquéd design in rosy red and green on white, then very finely quilted. This handsome quilt probably dates from between 1840 and 1890.

Introduction

The art and craft of American quiltmaking was born of the necessity for warm bed coverings among early settlers. As it developed, it transcended its humble beginnings and rose to artistic heights in the hands of these quilters. The forms used to express love of beauty and pride of workmanship were varied. From patchwork to appliqué to whole cloth, quilts were made in a myriad of patterns, colors, and fabrics. Contemporary quilters carry on the proud tradition, recording the lights and colors of their lives as they see them.

This book allows us a small glimpse into the fascinating quilts of our country. They are arranged in roughly chronological order, despite the pitfalls inherent in such ordering: Types of quilts were not popular everywhere at the same time, and quilters have always created individual patterns to suit themselves.

Each quilt here has its special appeal apart from time and place. Look for that as you celebrate beautiful quilts.

Left: *Blue and white quilts like* Orange Peel, *made in Ohio around 1840, are perennial favorites. Its effective use of dark and light allows the eye to play between blue- and white-edged circles. Right:* Rising Sun *is another difficult pattern with hundreds of small curving pieces. It is executed beautifully in this quilt made around 1860 by Eliza Ann Mattingly of Grayson Springs, Kentucky.*

Quilts—From Colonial to Contemporary

Early Quilts

Women in the American colonies made the same kinds of quilts as their European counterparts. With Independence came new styles of quilting—patchwork and appliquéd quilts that are uniquely American.

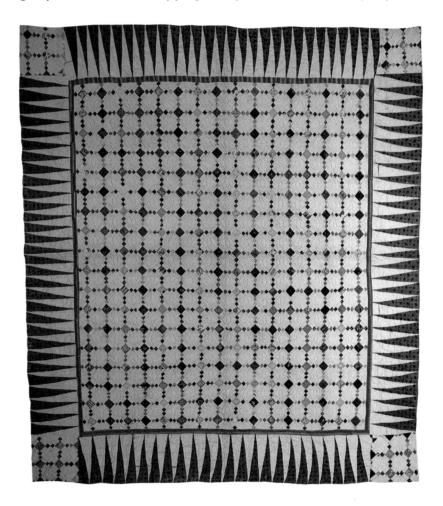

Left: Star is a very stylish quilt made around 1860 by Fannie Sales Trabue in Todd County, Kentucky. She carefully arranged the colors of its silks and velvets so that the star seems to radiate from the center. Above: A nine-patch square in Triangles and Patches is set on point with small squares touching, and the resulting voids are filled with light-colored solid fabric. This simple quilt was made in 1830 using very small scraps of cloth.

Early Quilts

Among the earliest surviving examples of fine colonial quilts were warmly padded linsey-woolsey whole cloths in solid colors. The best examples were beautifully quilted in thread matching their vibrant reds, greens, gold, or—more commonly—indigo. These quilts were usually not pieced except to join narrow fabrics into bedding width or to recycle the good parts from worn quilts. Made from either linen or cotton woven with wool, they were large, often reaching the floor from high colonial bedsteads. Worsteds and other woolens were also used for such quilts, since sleeping rooms were cold, and warm bed covers welcome.

Some of these wool quilts were divided at the corners to accommodate bedposts. Their fabric was often polished to a sheen (like the shine on a serge suit) by rubbing or through the application of various substances to create a glaze. Today, these early woolen quilts are found, for the most part, in museum collections.

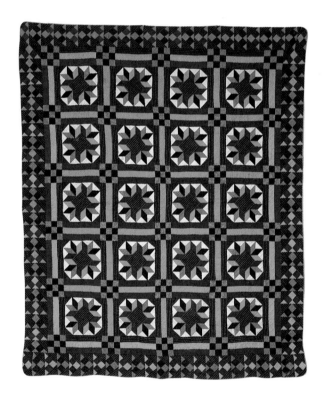

Left: Nine-Patch Crib *was made by a descendant of Squire Boone in Kentucky in 1834. Its relatively small size (34 × 48 inches) and large pieces make it a visually appealing project that could be made quickly.* Right: Doves at the Window with Flying Geese Border, *made in Kentucky circa 1860, is a beautifully planned and executed example of the American patchwork quilt. Both the cutting and piecing are virtually perfect.*

Quilts~From Colonial to Contemporary

This expertly pieced quilt called Stars in Garden Maze *is a model of balance and symmetry. Made around 1840 in Indiana, it has pleasantly open grillwork of dark strips that cover the entire piece. The small pieced star motifs are hung like jewels in their separate frames. This pieced and appliquéd quilt measures 68 × 80 inches.*

Quilts⁓From Colonial to Contemporary

Whigs' Defeat with Diamond Border *was made about 1840 by a member of the Powell family in Lawrence County, Tennessee. The piecing of the squares is quite exact, while the sashing is less perfectly matched. Perhaps the squares were pieced by a talented quilter and assembled, possibly at a later date, by one less gifted?*

Quilts~From Colonial to Contemporary

Early Quilts

Another specialty from the 18th century was white work. These were whole-cloth white quilts with a quilting design that covered the whole area. Traditionally, they had a top of finely woven cotton over a backing of loosely woven fabric like homespun, often with no batting layer between them. To raise areas of the overall quilting design, cotton batting or soft cording was stuffed between threads of the backing fabric by carefully parting it and then carefully closing it.

A similar method used a soft fabric to hold the stuffing under the parts of the design to be raised. The quilt was backed, with or without batting, and quilted to hold the "sandwich" together. The quilting was very fine, and the best white work quilts were among the most elegant examples of quilters' art. White work remained popular, especially in the South, to the Civil War and beyond, and is, in fact, still made today.

Left: White Trapunto Wreaths and Eagles with Fringe Border, *dated 1834, features a central medallion and a gracefully executed medallion border, which demonstrate why white work remains popular. It was made of cotton and kept for "best."* Above: Grape Vine, *a white work quilt, features a sinuous grapevine and corner baskets as border elements. Stuffed parts of the pattern give the composition texture and depth. This quilt was created around the middle of the 19th century.*

Quilts~From Colonial to Contemporary

Berries, Stems, and Flowers *has a lighthearted, ingenuous quality and is visually pleasing in both color and in the balance of the blocks and borders. It displays the red and green so popular when it was made (circa 1850). The Berries and Flowers motif, frequently present in appliqué quilts, is entirely original. The separation of the appliqué blocks by wide sashing sets them off to best advantage.*

Quilts~From Colonial to Contemporary

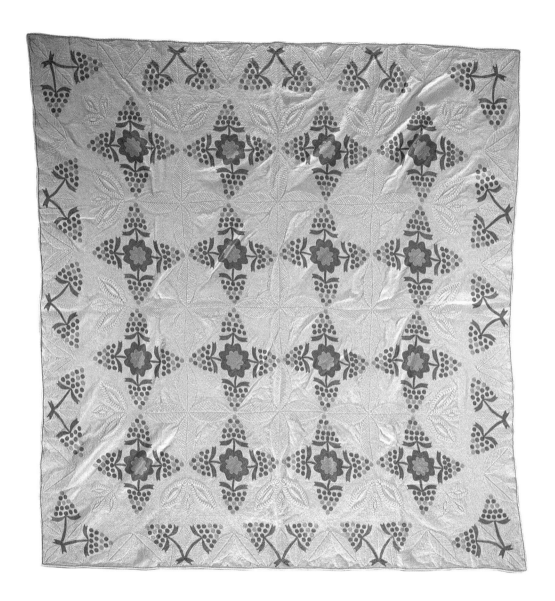

In this early Kentucky example (circa 1830) called Grapes and Flowers, the berries are grapes, and the flowers are not very detailed. The stipple quilting and bold trapunto motifs are a perfect counterpoint to the bright appliqué blocks and the bunches of "grapes" that make the border. Such quilts, combining fine quilting, stuffed work, and vibrant appliqué are the model of their type.

Quilts—From Colonial to Contemporary

*Sometime around the middle of the 19th century, Olive Batchelor Wells
made Garden of Eden from cotton, wool, and silk that she pieced, appliquéd,
embroidered, stuffed, gathered, beaded and, finally, quilted. Not surprisingly,
the inspiration for such a tour de force was the Bible. The appliqué
of grapevine, fruits, and flowers is particularly well done,
and the whole piece is finely quilted.*

Quilts~From Colonial to Contemporary

Fine quilting, delicate appliqué, and a sense of balance and control within the design characterize this Kentucky quilt called Cherry Trees. It was made of silk and velvet around the middle of the 19th century. Stuffed work adds emphasis and texture to a quilt that must have been reserved for special use and carefully preserved by successive owners from the time it was made.

Quilts~From Colonial to Contemporary

Early Quilts

American quilters developed both patchwork and appliqué to a high art by the middle of the 19th century. Where leisure and lovely fabrics were in good supply, as in wealthy plantation households, a showy kind of appliqué using printed motifs cut from chintz fabrics and appliquéd in artful arrangements on a plain white ground with borders, medallions, and even piecework was developed. This is now called *broderie perse*, which literally translates into "Persian embroidery." The inclusion of actual embroidery in the design was optional and infrequent.

This style was popular in England in the early 19th century, and a wealth of English chintzes came into America through the Eastern Seaboard ports. Some were printed with motifs designed to be cut out and used in *broderie perse*. The great *broderie perse* creations were often not quilted, but used as summer spreads, although some of the finest examples combine stuffed work and masterful quilting with the rich chintzes.

Left: *The maker of* Chintz Medallion *must have been a collector of chintzes who used very small bits to fashion a center medallion design surrounded by pieced and appliqué blocks.* Above (detail): Broderie Perse, *the art of reassembling printed motifs from floral chintzes as appliqué on a solid ground, represented the height of elegance in quiltmaking techniques in the first quarter of the 19th century when leisure and wealth supported it.*

Quilts~From Colonial to Contemporary

Carolina Lily, *popular around the middle of the 19th century,*
is a pieced pattern that gives the effect of appliqué. Here the "lilies" are
in pots and set in a grid of red sashes, alternating with what might be "suns"
to nourish the flowers. One block is set in the wrong direction, so as not
to offend God with perfection.

Quilts~From Colonial to Contemporary

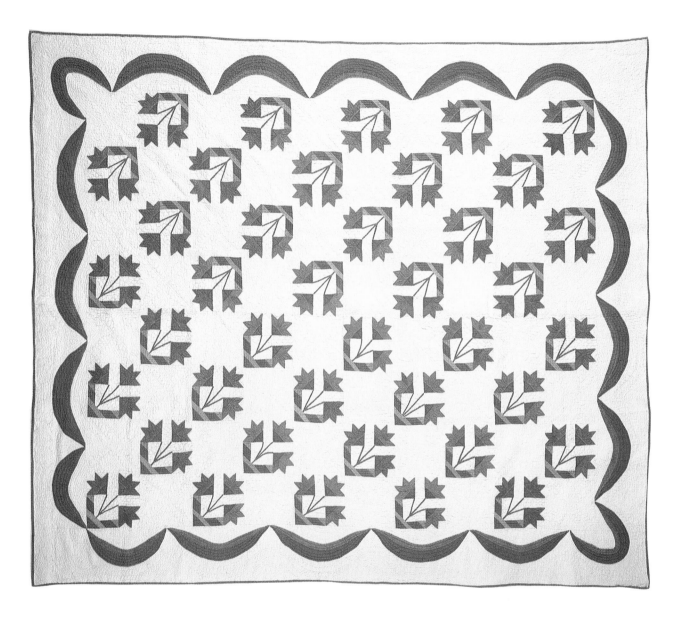

A Hart family member in Clark County, Kentucky, made North Carolina Lily, circa 1865. Though it is not visible in the photo, the quilter signed five family names in the quilting along one edge. She also showed consummate skill in the directional placement of the lily blocks and their relationship to the appliquéd border swags. One block faces in the wrong direction, guarding against arrogant perfection.

Quilts~From Colonial to Contemporary

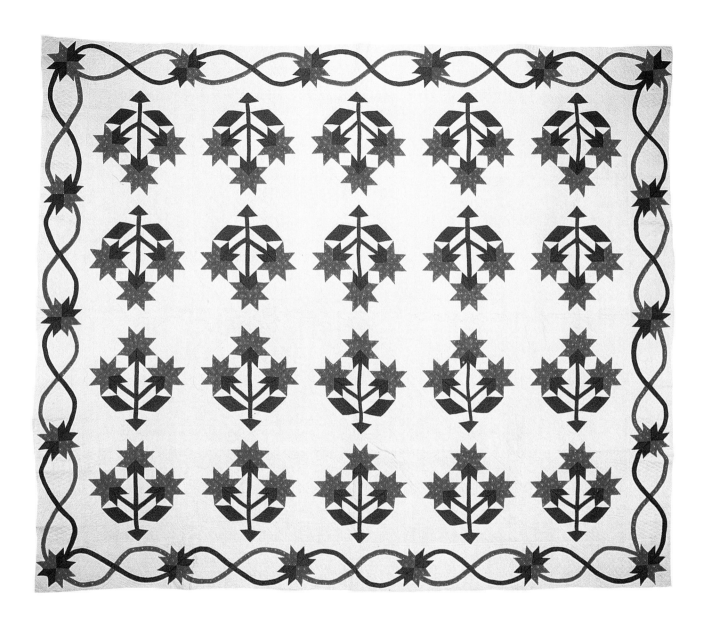

This variation of Carolina Lily is often called Peony, with its six petal segments representing the fuller blossoms of that plant. The appliqué Lily and Twist border is effective and finely executed on this Ohio quilt, circa 1840. The favored red, green, and orange-yellow color scheme probably added to the popularity of the pattern.

Quilts~From Colonial to Contemporary

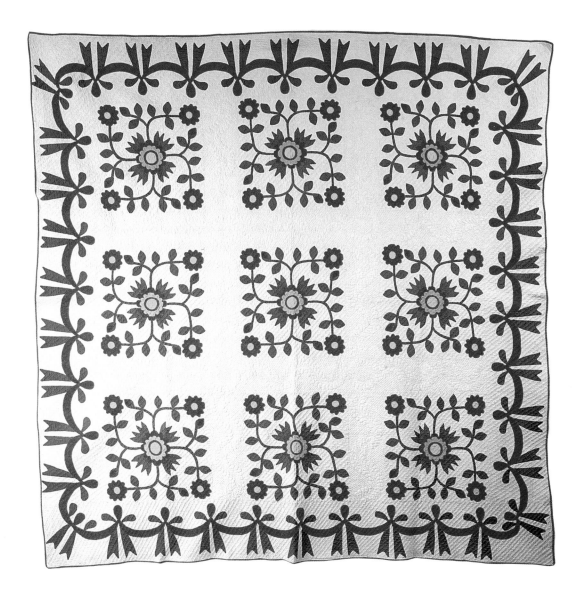

*This Ohio quilt, a Rose of Sharon Variation with a Swag/Bow Border,
is contained and orderly, with its appliqué blocks beautifully surrounded by the
elaborate border of swags and bows. The red, green, and orange-yellow
reinforce the mid-19th century dating of the quilt, when almost every quilter
made at least one appliqué production in these colors.*

Quilts~From Colonial to Contemporary

It was popular, especially in the South, to make *broderie perse* squares. Individual squares were produced by a friend or relative of a bride, or other fortunate recipient, and often signed in ink or embroidery, then set together with or without sashing. The resulting Friendship or Album quilt top was quilted (or at least quilting was begun) at a gathering of friends and well-wishers.

Appliqué, with the applied shapes cut either from solid color fabric or without regard to any printed design, was used widely to create lovely "best" or presentation quilts, including the Baltimore Album quilts. These glorious productions from that city made around 1840–1850 were generally considered the model for that type of work.

Appliqué quilts were made in every part of the country, even though their production required long hours for design and production. Sometimes appliqué was combined with patchwork or used as a border on a quilt made in a traditional pieced pattern.

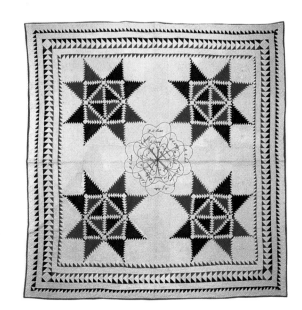

Left: *This Baltimore Album quilt was made in Maryland around 1854 by Susie Gorrel Harvey and her sister. Each square is beautifully planned to fill its space and is a treasure in its own right.*
Right: *Feathered Stars with Embroidered Friendship Center (circa 1860) would be a splendid production without its embroidered center block. By adding the names dear to her, the quilter combined memories with beauty and fine workmanship.*

Quilts~From Colonial to Contemporary

This Album *quilt is a true sampler, combining appliqué and pieced blocks outlined by narrow dark sashing. The squares seem to have been created by many hands; the appliqué representations of natural foliage and flowers run the gamut from realistic to stylized interpretation. Dated circa 1840, the quilt was made in Wisconsin and might have been quilted at a gathering of friends who contributed the blocks.*

Quilts~From Colonial to Contemporary

This sophisticated Album quilt boasts finely worked appliqué blocks that are coordinated in scale and color, then set together without contrasting sashing. The pieced border is an effective frame. Blocks are dated from 1844 to 1852, confirming the fact that friendship quilts often took a number of years to complete. Francina Stout Van Dyke is named the maker, and thus gets credit for bringing the project to conclusion.

Quilts~From Colonial to Contemporary

Late 19th Century Quilts

After the Civil War, bright cotton fabrics, cheaply manufactured in new textile mills, cheerful imported silks, and an emphasis on design over skillful stitchery enlivened American quiltmaking.

Left: A Pennsylvania quilter made Garfield and Arthur by surrounding a political bandanna with star rays for emphasis. She was probably a seamstress or upholsterer to have such a stunning array of chintz prints. Above: In Centennial Flag, 39-star flags of 1876 dominate all other banners in the corners, and a centennial commemorative bandanna forms the centerpiece. Esther Elizabeth Cooley of Massachusetts pieced this quilt in that year.

Nine-Patch Postage Stamp Miniature *uses a simple, adaptable block and the smallest scraps to create interesting patterns. Here, the blocks are unusually small; it takes 480 alternating with white solid blocks to fill this quilt's central field. Contrasting dark and light fabrics are used effectively in blocks and occur again in the borders, where a myriad of colorful bits pieced together on the square frame this quilt made in Kentucky around 1870.*

Quilts~From Colonial to Contemporary

Hexagonal piecing, an English tradition and early 19th century fashion, was usually seen in a whole pattern or as small clusters of "flowers." In Honeycomb, *it creates a central motif in pleasing and skillfully placed colors. Kentuckian Sophronia Ann Bruce made this quilt circa 1880. Stuffed work in the unusual appliqué border and elaborate quilting add the crowning touches to a highly original creation of cotton, wool, and silk.*

Quilts~From Colonial to Contemporary

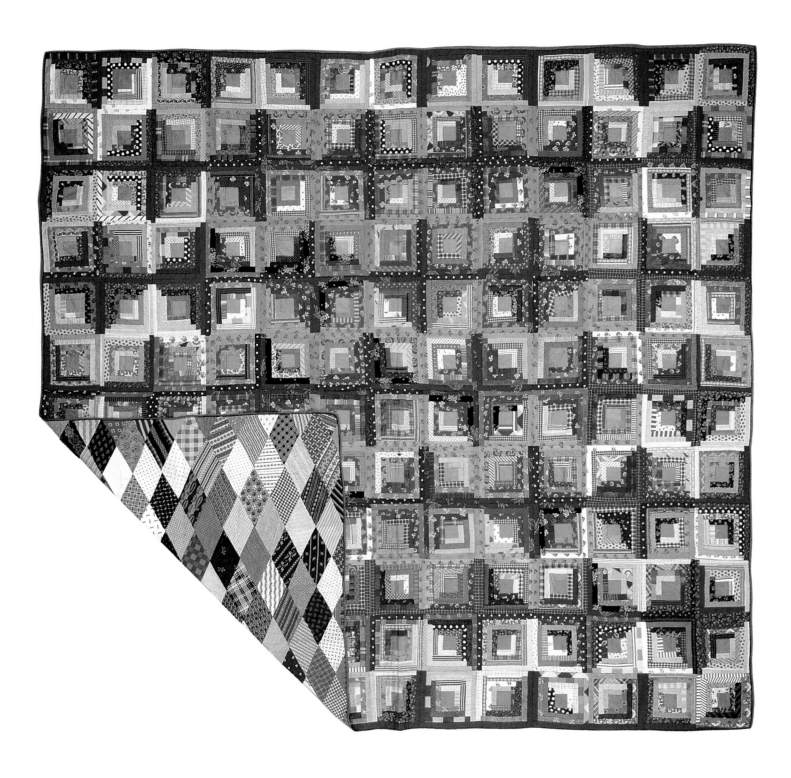

Late 19th Century Quilts

Patchwork patterns spread rapidly throughout the 19th century. They crossed the country in covered wagons and shaped the final scraps of frontier wardrobes into warm and often beautiful bed covers. As the country became settled, rural quilters joined their urban counterparts in creating what became the stunning body of artistic output we call American patchwork quilts.

Patchwork was standard for utilitarian quilts. They were assembled from materials at hand in the simplest patterns or in no pattern at all. Most utility quilts are gone now. Once they became too worn for bed covers, they became pallets for children playing or sleeping on the floor, and ended up as rags around the homestead.

Log Cabin and its variations were probably the typical pieced quilts of the 19th century. The half-light, half-dark squares made Courthouse Steps, Barn Raising, Straight Furrow, and many other patterns, depending on how they were set together. Log Cabin remains popular with quilters today.

Left: Reversible Log Cabin/Diamond Back *uses the Streak of Lightning set for the "log" blocks on one side, then has a backing pieced from diamond shapes. This reversible quilt uses the same range of color and prints on both sides.* Right: Log Cabin Barn Raising with Multiple Borders *is a dramatic Log Cabin variation that contrasts solid red with a deliberately created striped pattern in the other half of each block.*

Quilts~From Colonial to Contemporary

A *Straight Furrow* Log Cabin was seldom used as a Friendship quilt,
but this one was made and signed by Ohio friends of Anthony and
Matilda Charlotte Coler as a gift on the occasion of their moving to Kansas
in 1884. The fact that it was never used, but handed down through five
generations of the family, indicates how it was treasured by both the recipients
and their descendants.

Quilts~From Colonial to Contemporary

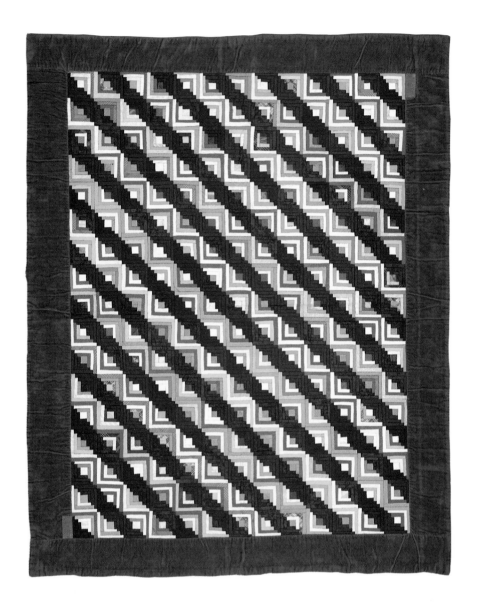

Quilts made of small pieces have a kind of universal appeal, and this 48 × 58-inch Log Cabin is no exception. It is dated March 4, 1889, and celebrates the inauguration of Benjamin Harrison as President, bearing a tag "Souvenir Inaugural Ball." Perhaps its narrow strips of silk and velvet were scraps of ball gowns, a memento for those who wore them. They may also have been collected by a seamstress who dressed many fashionable women.

Quilts~From Colonial to Contemporary

37

Clean, sharp images and skillful stippled quilting accented with trapunto (stuffed work) are evident in this Kentucky quilt called Touching Stars made in the last quarter of the 19th century. The bold design of the four stars contained within the doubled framing borders gives this quilt the visual impact of a modern graphic. It looks deceptively simple to achieve, but without perfect piecing, the effect is easily spoiled.

Quilts~From Colonial to Contemporary

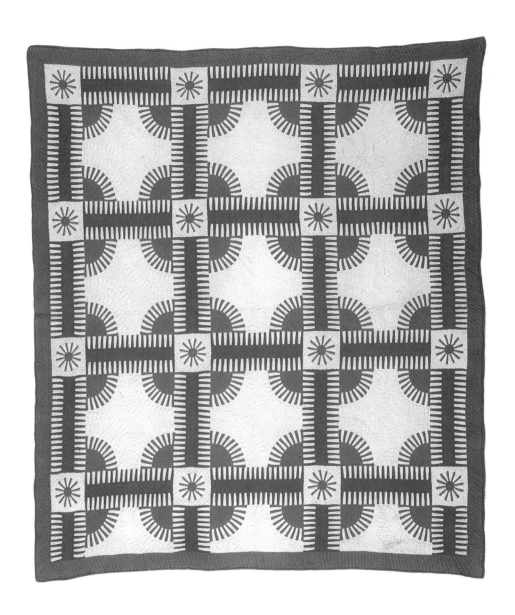

New York Beauty *is one of the pieced patterns that should be undertaken
only by a skilled quilter who has the patience to strive for perfection.
Mistakes in the intricate piecing tend to be immediately obvious to the viewer.
Made in Kentucky about 1875, this example is somewhat unusual in its use
of the half block at one end, which probably was meant for the top of the bed
under pillow shams.*

Quilts~From Colonial to Contemporary

Late 19th Century Quilts

Victorian Crazy Quilts represented the essence of an era famous for its quilt design. From roughly 1880 to about 1910–20, they symbolized needlework at its fashionable finest.

Memorabilia was high fashion in quilting—from souvenir-printed patches to silk tobacco pouches and miniature flags. Also popular were opulent fabrics like taffetas, satins, and velvets; embellishments such as embroidery, lace, ribbons, and appliqué showed up almost anywhere. Motifs were varied. They ran from sweet flowers, rainbows, birds and nests, animals and their young to solemn urns, memorial shields, and even caskets. Mortality weighed heavily on the Victorian mind. Almost inappropriately, there was also a half-risqué sprinkling of garters, boots, and bloomers associated with the Gay '90s.

All of these motifs were used in Victorian Crazy Quilts. Sometimes they were used all at once on the same quilt. Victorian Crazy Quilts were seldom quilted and were used on top of plain white bed coverings. Backed with a soft and luxurious fabric, they were also decorative throws meant for display in public rooms of the house or to drape a genteel lap against a draft.

Left: Made in Louisville, Kentucky, around 1880, this pieced Crazy Quilt *features briar stitching where the pieces join and elaborate embroidery and appliqué elsewhere on the varied fabrics. Right: This detail of the* Crazy Quilt *on the opposite page shows one of its appealing little ladies dressed in her cap, apron, and dainty puffed-sleeved gown. It was typical for Crazy Quilts to be virtually encrusted with embroidery and appliqué.*

Quilts~From Colonial to Contemporary

Probably the best thing about a Crazy Quilt was the fun of making it—collecting fabrics, putting them together, then embellishing the creation. The process involved exchanging bits of fabric among friends and family, designing appropriate representations of memorable events in one's life, and sewing on the pieces during long and pleasant sessions of gossip and refreshments. The name may have derived from the "crazing" of ceramic glazes with random, sharply angled lines, which the random piecing of Crazy Quilts suggested.

Crazy Quilts were a scrapbook, a conversation piece. Today, we marvel at the amount of work lavished on these items fashioned from such im-

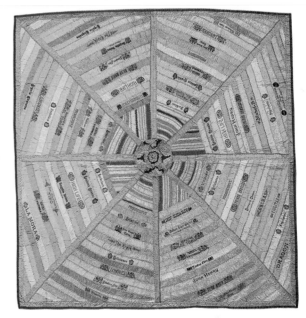

practical fabrics. Crazies that are literally disintegrating are all too common, providing a lesson to quilters about choosing durable fabrics to carry their stitches to posterity. The disintegration of many Victorian Crazy Quilts today is a fitting epitaph to a society preoccupied with death and dying.

Left: Old Homestead Crazy *is an example of a Crazy Quilt where careful framing and a relatively limited range of piece sizes help avoid an utterly random look.* Above: *Silk cigar bands were used to make this small (35 × 36-inch) Kentucky quilt. The narrow strips are placed in an imaginative composition and great effort is lavished on fragile fabric. Certainly, however,* Cigar Bands, *was, and is, a curiosity.*

Quilts—From Colonial to Contemporary

Crazy Quilt, *an example of the Contained Crazy, seems almost inappropriately named. You must study it to see that it is divided into large squares pieced of silk and velvet, which were joined together after they were suitably embellished. Kentuckian Lizzie Hollinger made and dated this quilt in 1885. Besides incredible amounts of embroidery, she added the novelty of three-dimensional work to her large (86 × 103-inch) creation.*

Quilts~From Colonial to Contemporary

A simple Nine-Patch block was used to create this elegant crib quilt,
made of silk and decorated with briar stitching. The simplicity of Nine-Patch
Crib *sets off the richness of the fabric in a way that Crazy Quilts, with*
their busy piling of pattern on pattern, could not. Since this was made
in Kentucky around 1880 at the height of Crazy Quilt fashion, its maker
showed commendable restraint.

Quilts—From Colonial to Contemporary

Six-inch pieced or appliquéd blocks are joined and unified by sashing marked
with red squares. This charming Sampler is named Hearts and
Hands, *which the devout dedicate to God. (See inset.) Hearts appear
frequently in the traditional artwork of Pennsylvania, where this quilt was
made near the end of the last century. Many other Christian symbols—crosses,
stars, and the dove of peace—also appear in this quilt.*

Quilts~From Colonial to Contemporary

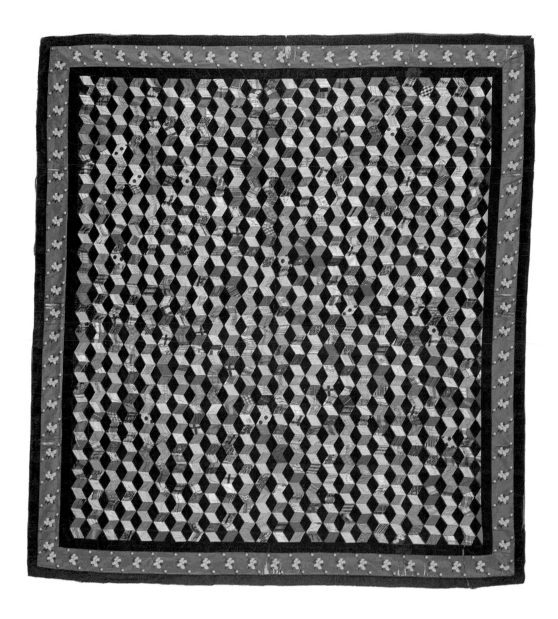

Optical illusion can be achieved through the choice and placement of dark versus light tones in a design. Baby's Blocks, or Tumbling Blocks, is an example of an ancient arrangement of diamonds in three color tones. It was a favorite of American quilters when this silk and velvet quilt was pieced around 1870 by Julia Wickliffe Beckham, daughter of a Kentucky governor. The delicate floral border is a suitable frame.

Quilts~From Colonial to Contemporary

Late 19th Century Quilts

Hawaiian quilts represent another distinct and unmistakable quilting style. Native island women, first taught to quilt by missionaries to Polynesia, soon began to create their own remarkable designs. Most featured appliqué patterns that covered the whole quilt top in a solid, brilliant color against a solid background.

Perhaps these early island quilts should be called Polynesian quilts, since those made on the island of Tahiti were related in design, color, and technique. According to some authorities, they were actually made earlier than the earliest Hawaiian pieces. The similarity of fabrics was no surprise, since both cultures used the cotton trade goods that came with the missionaries to replace the traditional tapa cloth made from processed and painted sheets of bark. There was also a period prior to 1900 when production centered on red, white, and blue flag quilts, which are especially prized by collectors.

Even though the large-scale graphics of the Hawaiian or Polynesian quilts look very contemporary, the first were produced early in the 19th century. Their style is still in vogue, and they are still made today.

Left: *Quilts featuring the Hawaiian flag and royal coat of arms were popular in the second half of the 19th century, and the Union Jack in* Hawaiian Flag Quilt *indicates close ties to the British Empire.*
Right: *Red and white are popular colors for Hawaiian quilts (such as in* Hawaiian Red and White Quilt) *featuring the paper-cutting appliqué techniques thought to have been introduced by Western missionaries.*

Quilts~From Colonial to Contemporary

Late 19th Century Quilts

According to undocumented oral tradition, slaves who were talented seamstresses made or helped to make quilts. The African-American quilts, lately recognized as artistically distinct, are those that were made in black families for their own use and represent a separate part of our culture. Such quilts were made quite early in the 19th century, but because they saw hard use, few dating before the late 19th century have survived.

African-American quilts form a loosely related group. Most show a strong sense of design and a sure handling of color even on the most coarsely quilted, utilitarian quilts. The quiltmakers often pieced traditional patterns, but varied them in interesting ways. Many, however, were original designs using available fabrics. Some of the most striking quilts featured large pieces of random size and shape arranged in bold compositions.

Left: *This 1860 appliqué production, made by slave Mahulda Mize in Kentucky, was probably little used through the years to judge by its bright colors. Called* Princess Feather with Oak Leaves, *the pattern derives from the Prince of Wales' insignia. Above: Biblical inspiration is a common thread in African-American quilt history, and obvious in this Georgia quilt made around 1900.* Bible Scenes *illustrates the Fall of Man and the Crucifixion.*

Quilts~From Colonial to Contemporary

Early 20th Century Quilts

The economic chaos during the first half of the 20th century brought about a resurgence of the simple art of quiltmaking, with many American quilters adding their own personal embellishments to traditional patterns.

Left: *To commemorate the 200th anniversary of George Washington's birth, Carrie Hall made the* George Washington Bicentennial Quilt *in 1932. She adapted its central motif from a pattern in a syndicated newspaper column and added a frame of blocks in a pattern called Washington Pavement.*
Above: *In* Spools with Six Borders, *the color in the spools against the white background lets the eye switch between the image of spools and that of white pinwheels against a red ribbon grid.*

Resembling a contemporary graphic or a series of posterized photographs, Cows was made in Kentucky around 1900 by a quilter with a sense of humor as well as a sense of design. Both piecing and appliqué are used, and the rather coarse and strongly vertical lines of widely spaced quilting seem an integral part of the composition.

Quilts~From Colonial to Contemporary

The boldness and definition of the red and white piecework almost overpower the delicate lines of the embroidered motifs that border the central panel in Red and White Stars. Red and white quilts enjoyed a vogue in the early years of this century when this Kentucky quilt was made. Patterns for blocks to be embroidered with flowers, birds, etc., were available commercially, but these may be original, judging by the names given to the embroidered figures.

Quilts—From Colonial to Contemporary

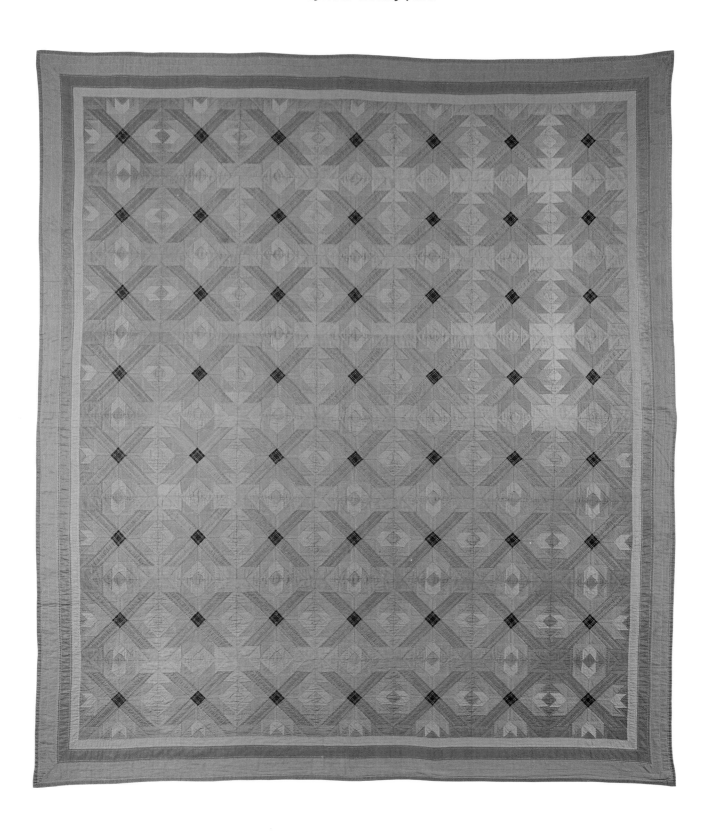

Members of the Amish sect share a religious conviction that traditionally has kept their worldly possessions simple, quietly colored, and functional, but allowed all their love of color and artistic talent to shine through in the bold geometric patterns and brilliant hues of their quilts. Their descendants in rural Ohio, Indiana, and Pennsylvania continue to produce quilts in traditional patterns and colors. Many of these quilts are sold to support community causes.

Most of the finest and most collectible examples date from about the middle of the 19th century through the third decade of the 20th. The quilting on early examples is often incredibly fine, with the large areas of solid color illustrating to perfection these types of quilts. The strong graphic elements and use of color in Amish quilts have influenced contemporary design in many areas.

When the Roaring '20s passed and deepening economic depression settled over the country, women took to their needles and revived the half-forgotten art of quilting. They fashioned the remnants of prosperity into beautiful and comfortable quilts in a time of trouble.

Left: *The deft use of glowing color, the fine piecing, and beautiful quilting are all typically Amish characteristics of* Cross and Crown *made in Indiana around 1930.* Right: *Referred to as an* Amish Plain Quilt, *this possesses the sort of "plainness" that shows off beautiful quilt stitches. Proportion, color, and quilting are all first class, and combine to produce a lovely bed cover in this Ohio quilt.*

Quilts~From Colonial to Contemporary

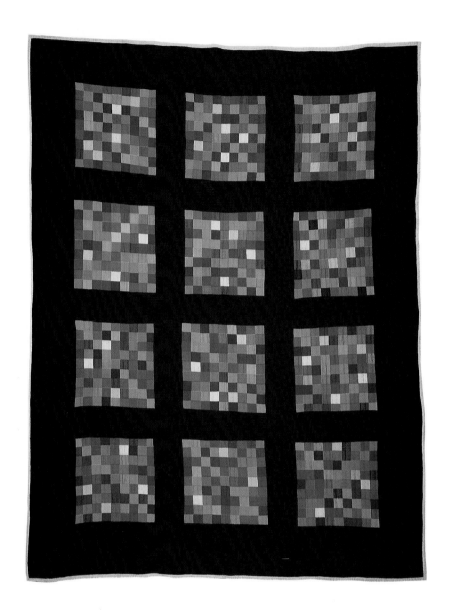

Like bits of stained glass back lit in a dark frame, these pieced blocks, composed of 81 patches each, glow with jewellike colors. Note the careful placement of colors to achieve the rose and blue X across each multicolored block. 81 Patch is Ohio Amish (circa 1930), which experts in the field distinguish from Amish quilts of the Pennsylvania type illustrated on the facing page.

Quilts~From Colonial to Contemporary

This quilt (circa 1920) distills the essence of Pennsylvania Amish design. Simplicity, boldness of scale, and the pure deep colors in unexpected combinations have influenced the arts far beyond the realm of quilting. In such masterful quilts as this wool Diamond in a Square, *there is always some small surprise; here it is the four bright squares where the blue and green borders of the center intersect at the corners.*

Quilts~From Colonial to Contemporary

Looking like a modern interpretation of the old Log Cabin pattern, this Amish Log Cabin was made around 1940 in Somerset County, Pennsylvania. The "logs" are three equal strips pieced to the block, and the Barn Raising set is used. The simple blocks make a very effective design, which is enhanced by the typically Amish use of pastels as a foil for black. The blue inner border is an expert touch.

Quilts~From Colonial to Contemporary

Wonderful sunset-to-dark colors of cotton pieced in the subtle stripes of Joseph's Coat set apart this Pennsylvania Mennonite quilt made around the turn of the century. The border undeniably makes the quilt, repeating the series of shading from a different angle, giving both movement and containment to the whole composition. Mennonite and Amish quilt designs are related, but there are subtle differences.

Quilts~From Colonial to Contemporary

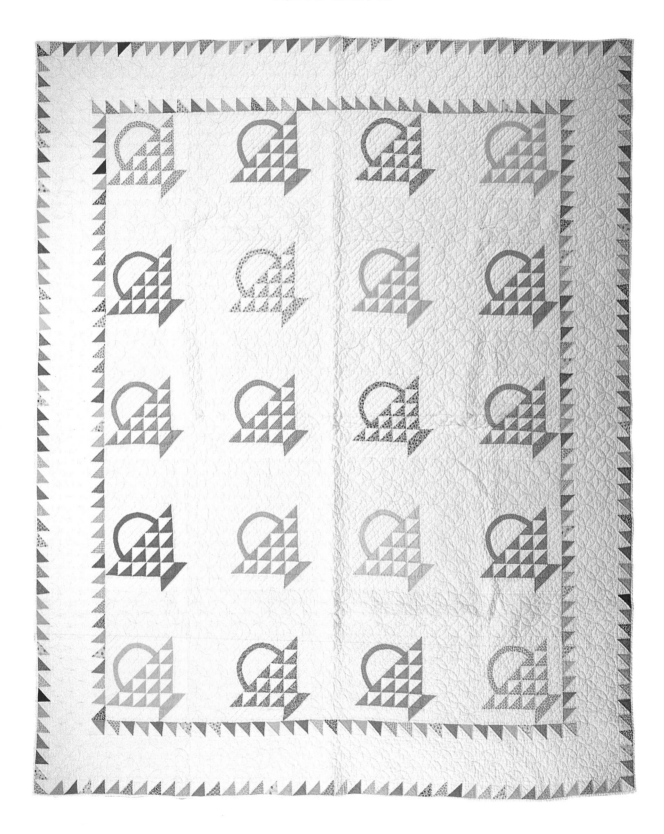

Early 20th Century Quilts

The generation of quilters coming of age during the Depression was the first in the history of the country that had not learned needlework at mother's knee. Fortunately, there were enough grandmothers and aunts of an age to remember, and some who still quilted. They became an important resource for the new "make-do" generation.

What we call Depression quilts today were not made by the migrating families forced off farms by financial calamity. They were fashioned by those who were able to stay at home in strained financial circumstances. Scrap quilts were a challenging way to make useful and pretty bed coverings economically.

Frequently, quilters could purchase cotton prints and solids, which were inexpensive even by Depression standards. Soft pastels or "flower colors" were favored, especially when combined with white.

Left: *Dainty piecing and pastels on white mark* Baskets *as a product of the 1930s. The pieced baskets are more exacting than the solid triangles often used beneath the curved "handle" in quicker, easier versions of this popular pattern.* Right: *The pieced blocks with* Chinese Lanterns *use many varied cotton prints to best advantage and are an ideal pattern for a scrap quilt. This typical Depression-era quilt might have been derived from newspaper or magazine sources.*

Quilts~From Colonial to Contemporary

Thousands of tiny fabric triangles are pieced to make this traditional eight-pointed Postage Stamp Star on a 59 × 70-inch quilt. The miniaturization of the pieces gives a special textural quality, and would have allowed this 1930s Kentucky quilter to use the smallest scrap in the bag. The precise arrangement of the colors, which groups the lights and darks so that the star radiates, is a testimony to the creativity of quilters.

Quilts~From Colonial to Contemporary

Some quilts possess more novelty than aesthetic value; this Miniature Postage Stamp *has both. Made in the 1920s in Kentucky, it contains over 16,500 tiny pieces fashioned, row on row, into 42 Postage Stamp blocks. "No scrap too small," might have been the quilter's motto, and one would like to know how long it took to finish this interesting piece and whether its maker ever undertook another!*

Quilts—From Colonial to Contemporary

Stars pieced out to hexagons, then placed in rows to form concentric hexagons, radiate like ripples on a pond from the central star in this unusual Kentucky quilt dated 1934. The fabrics are appropriate for the time, but the design of Hexagonal Stars seems a bit more structured and formal than was common in quilts made for daily use. Perhaps its maker planned it as a fair entry?

Quilts~From Colonial to Contemporary

Called Star of France *because the design was inspired by a Napoleonic medal, this pieced cotton quilt was made in Ohio around 1930. It is precise in design and execution, with very exacting piecing. The choice of colors, scale, symmetry, and placement of the Star figure within the gold and pink borders produces a very formal, yet graphically stimulating, quilt.*

Quilts~From Colonial to Contemporary

Early 20th Century Quilts

Patchwork was popular, but flowers and fruits appliquéd in exquisite garlands and clusters on solid ground were the jewels of the Depression-era quilts. The whole pattern was finely quilted and often featured stuffed work. Some of the finest seem to have been original designs, but many were offered as commercially produced kits, which are being reproduced and sold again today.

An endearing aspect of quilts of this era was the prevalence of child-inspired patterns. Sunbonnet Sue led the list, but her Overall Sam companion, joined by a menagerie of both copied and original animals, appeared with charming frequency. These quilts were both a joy and comfort to children and an inexpensive gift of love from family quilters.

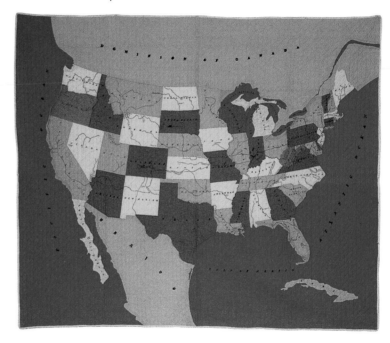

Left: *This charming appliqué quilt, called* A Curiosity Bedspread, *was made for a Sears Roebuck contest by Mrs. Avery Burton in Mississippi. Its imaginative use of fabric for the various animals should have won an important prize for its maker.* Above: *Somewhere in Indiana in the 1920s, a quilter seized a child's geography book and designed a quilt from its map. It was probably made as a fair or contest entry.*

Quilts~From Colonial to Contemporary

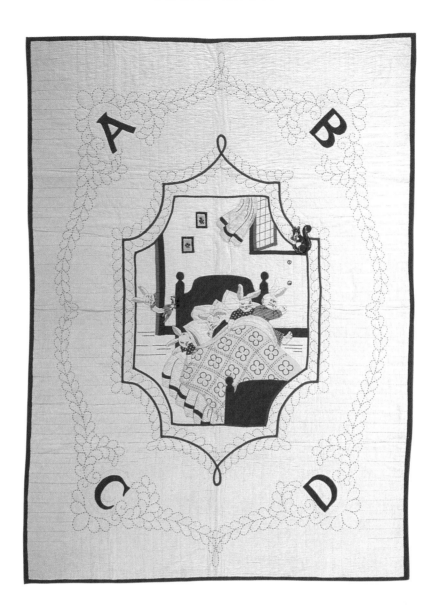

The intricate appliqué scene that centers Rabbits in Bed (49 × 67 inches) has the look of a professional illustration and was probably part of a kit or commercial pattern, which were widely available around 1940 when it was made. The needlework is very fine, and the use of red thread for the quilting nicely echoes the red letters and binding.

Quilts—From Colonial to Contemporary

Mother-in-Law *on her flowery walk seems dwarfed by the large house and rather threatening trees in this appliqué quilt. Made in Missouri by Lulu Bennett around 1930, the quilt was perhaps a gift for the relative she depicted. Pictorial quilts enjoy a certain perennial popularity, but the frame-filling quality of this example is unusual. The zigzag edge, nicely bound and turned at the corners, is effective in the composition.*

Quilts~From Colonial to Contemporary

This Rose Tree *appliqué design from the 19th century was given a dramatic Swag and Bowknot border treatment by its maker, Rose Good Kretsinger, working in Emporia, Kansas, in 1929. Her appliqué is flawless and the quilting as fine as any in the antique quilts she loved. She is most widely known, however, as co-author of* The Romance of the Patchwork Quilt *with Carrie Hall.*

Quilts~From Colonial to Contemporary

This original design by Rose Good Kretsinger defines the genre of pastel, floral Depression-era quilts. The border is her graceful invention, based on the cable quilting design, and the quilting is exquisite. An orchid pictured on an advertising card inspired this quilt, which was completed in 1929 after two years of work. Orchid Wreath won many prizes.

Quilts~From Colonial to Contemporary

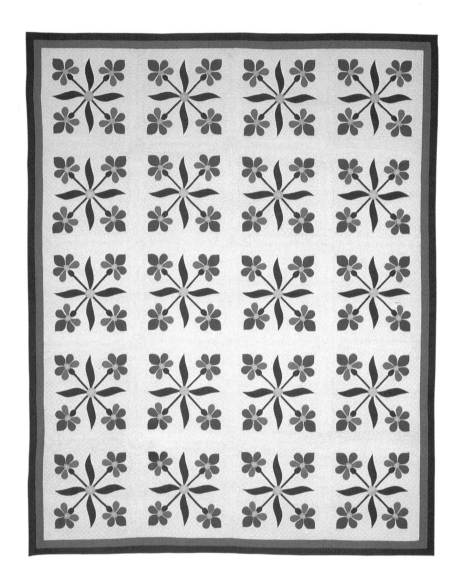

Floral quilts of the 1920s can be quite stylized, such as Iris, a crisp appliqué made in Kansas by Mary M. Stayman. Varying shades of violet and lavender add much to its impact. At the time, widely available commercial patterns gave quilts a professional look, providing the quilter was skillful. Mrs. Stayman's execution is perfect, and her quilting very fine, despite the general decline in that art since the turn of the century.

Quilts~From Colonial to Contemporary

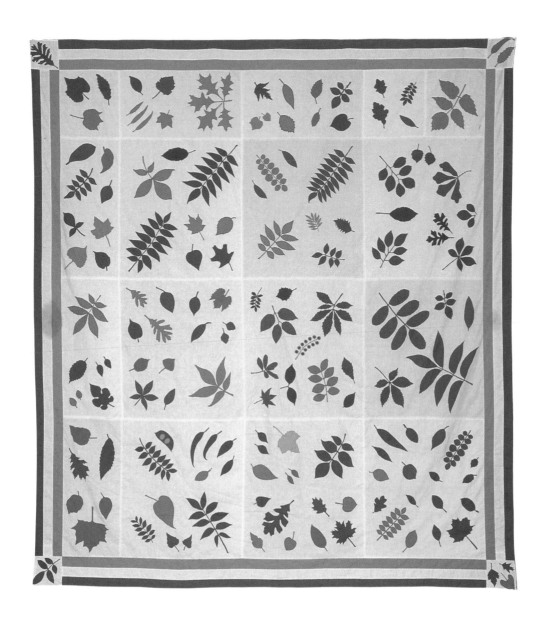

Leaf, *an unbacked summer spread, was made by Mary M. Stayman in 1923 (her* Iris *quilt is shown opposite). Her father, a noted horticulturist, inspired her interest in plants. She wrote the name of each of the 122 different leaves on the reverse of this spread. At least one similar unbacked summer spread with botanically correct leaves appliquéd in green on a white background exists.*

Quilts—From Colonial to Contemporary

Overall Sam, *quilted companion of Sunbonnet Sue, is one of the endearing, child-inspired patterns of the Depression. Many variants were published or drawn by quilters and passed around to friends. In this example, made in Kentucky around 1930, the use of colored background blocks interspersed with white and the pieced border contribute design interest. Quilts like this provided beauty and warmth to children of the time.*

Quilts~From Colonial to Contemporary

Pictorial quilts date from many periods, but few are as detailed as Sunday School Picnic. The appliquéd border—a dainty parade of little girls all dressed up—is charming next to the central panel of the Sunday School picnic. This wonderful quilt, dated 1932, was made in Pennsylvania by Jennie C. Trein. It measures 84 × 82 inches, and was probably made strictly for display.

Quilts~From Colonial to Contemporary

Contemporary Quilts

Today American quiltmaking includes exquisite traditional quilts, elaborate art quilts, beautifully designed pieces that blend needlework with other media, and emotionally charged group-made quilts.

Left: North Country *is a 45 × 45-inch piece based on an original design by Massachusetts artist Mary Lou Smith, and was pieced and quilted by hand by Ruth M. Norton. Its carefully chosen colors and fabrics symbolize winter in the North. Above:* Tornado I *is the first of a three-quilt series (see page 88 for another) by Merrill Mason that uses the tornado as a metaphor for physical and emotional turmoil.*

Patriotic sentiments ran high just before World War II when Flag and Liberty Bell was made. Its designer created a powerful graphic, flanking the symbolic bell with a flag with the original 13 stars and another 38-star version. The eccentric arrangement on the field of the latter may have been dictated by the desired star size or by some special significance that now escapes us. Large-scale star blocks and red borders balance this quilt.

In 1980 Jesse Telfair pieced this quilt that leaves no doubt about its message. Large scale alphabet motifs have been used to create quilt designs in the past, but seldom more successfully than in this stunning example, entitled Freedom. Consider the loss, visually, had white been chosen for the background color of this spectacular quilt.

Quilts~From Colonial to Contemporary

Whoever produced Ike around 1950 was perhaps more of a partisan than a quilter, judging by the haphazard directional placement of the Eisenhower campaign bandannas. It would have been just as easy, and more visually pleasing, to use the strong arcs created by the letters in a symmetrical way. This is an interesting memento of the times. Its historical value will probably increase more swiftly than its value as needlework.

Quilts~From Colonial to Contemporary

Contemporary Quilts

The revival of quilting in the Depression era was based largely on economic need. When women went back to the workplace during World War II, extra money became available for household decorative items. However, quilting declined in popularity since the newer members of the work force had no time to devote to it. Some women continued to quilt, but it was not a skill handed down from mother to daughter. Gradually, it became almost a novelty to know someone who made quilts.

The "Abstract Design in American Quilts" exhibit at New York's Whitney Museum in 1971 is generally credited with rekindling an interest in quilts and quilting in the United States. It confirmed a growing need to look at our past, and this search for roots brought a new appreciation of old quilts. As these came out of closets and chests and into antique shops and museum collections, their growing material value reinforced their cultural worth, and quilting was "in" again.

Left: *Judith A. Montaño teaches the Crazy Quilt technique internationally. She believes C.Q. has such wide appeal because it makes a beautiful and unique repository for memorabilia, as* Crazy Quilt Friends *demonstrates.* Above: *Michael Cummings created a three-part series on* Haitian Boat People *(this is II) in response to TV scenes of the refugees seeking freedom. It took about six months to complete this 60 × 96-inch piece in appliqué using hot Caribbean colors and touches of textile paint.*

Quilts—From Colonial to Contemporary

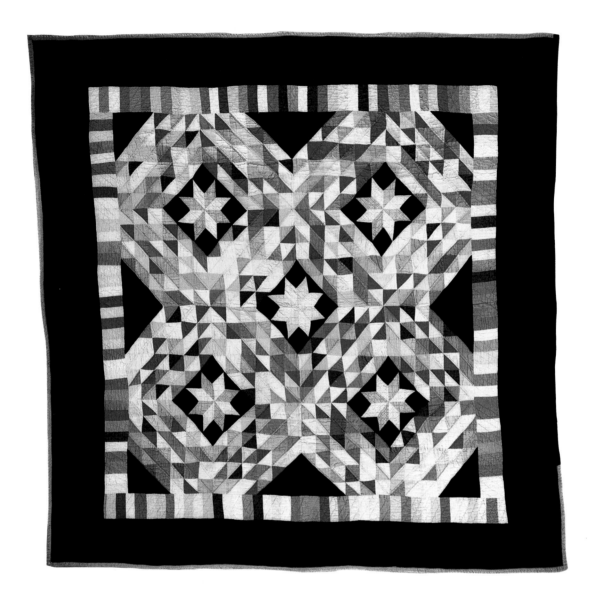

Amish Ocean Waves with Stars was made around 1940 in Holmes County, Ohio, and typically shows the influence of other quilt traditions often apparent in later Amish work. Expert piecing, deft handling of color, value, and scale, plus the effective contrast of black, are evidence of its Amish quilting heritage. The Ocean Waves pattern framework and the five large stars seem suspended against the black background as against the midnight sky.

Quilts~From Colonial to Contemporary

In this 45 × 56-inch wall quilt, City Lights, *the traditional Ohio Star is transformed by Joan Rigal, a contemporary Ohio quilter influenced by Amish quilts. This influence shows in the expert juxtaposition of rich colors set off by black and the small surprise of the yellow-green points sparkling around the outside. She began quilting with a museum class in 1980, and this 1986 piece is the first she submitted to a juried show.*

Quilts—From Colonial to Contemporary

Contemporary Quilts

The new generation of quilters tends to "group" in quilting classes, clubs, or guilds. They also travel to seminars, workshops, and symposia to enjoy the social aspects of quiltmaking as they strive to become more proficient in the craft.

Many have time-consuming careers and can only take classes at night or on weekends. However, they spend dollars on their hobby that would amaze their quilting ancestors, and have rejuvenated the market for cotton piece goods and a plethora of quilting paraphernalia.

The Sampler quilt is probably the hallmark of the current revival. Individual blocks are pieced in the same fabric combinations, with each in a different traditional quilt pattern. These blocks are set together in a unifying grid of sashing and borders. Quilting teachers find this a way to teach a lot of piecing techniques in a short time, and thousands of Sampler quilts have been made. The Log Cabin quilt, easily adaptable to machine piecing, is another very popular classroom pattern.

Left: Heritage *is a wedding quilt for a son and his wife in which Lois Tornquist Smith captured family history and memories. A year in the making, this prize-winning Sampler was completed in 1987.*
Right: *This* Friendship Sampler *is a collection of pieced quilt block patterns and a valuable index to fabrics in use at the time of its construction around 1940 in Ohio. Names of friends are signed on the blocks.*

Quilts~From Colonial to Contemporary

Contemporary Quilts

Artists working in other media could not ignore quilting for long. Since the 1970s, art quilts have become an important part of the quilting scene. By definition, an art quilt is a decorative piece or wall hanging, as opposed to one designed for use as, for example, a bed covering. Whether or not it is art constitutes a subjective judgment, but it should be remembered that not even old quilts are uniformly appealing to all viewers.

The finest of contemporary art quilts are splendid in their use of color, fabric, and the techniques of appliqué, patchwork, stuffed quilting, machine, and hand work. Even painting and photography are pressed into service. Contemporary quilts are varied. They may be subtle and restful in their effects or bold, graphic, and forceful. They represent an evolving aspect of quilting, which is as fascinating as any in its history.

Left: Tornado III *by Merrill Mason seems totally unrelated to the initial piece (shown on page 79), until one discovers the tornado photograph motif laser-copied and heat-transferred onto the back. Above: Like many traditional quilt designs, Merrill Mason's* Postcard Quilt *uses a simple repeat block with a border, but the hand-printed fabric, photocopied postcard images, and lettered borders set it apart. The postcards are mementos of Mason's travels as a museum administrator.*

Quilts~From Colonial to Contemporary

Clare M. Murray says she can never enter a fabric store without touching every bolt. In Travelog #3 (measuring 65 × 65 inches), her fascination with textiles combines with the appeal of architectural, three-dimensional images. It is easy to "get inside" this piece, following the "stairs," entering the "doorways," and walking the "pavements." The crisply pieced quilt blocks emphasize the architectural quality of quilt patterns.

Quilts~From Colonial to Contemporary

In her Travelog series, quilt artist Clare M. Murray uses hand and machine piecing and appliqué to explore the relationship of various design elements in space and to translate architectural forms into fabric. In this 76 × 100-inch piece, she is representing the cobblestone streets she encountered in Europe and the open sky. A self-taught quilter since 1980, Murray works six to eight hours a day at her art.

Quilts~From Colonial to Contemporary

"Black earth and the bright colors of new life" were the inspiration for Jane Sassaman's Garden Spiral. The Chicago quilt artist used repeat blocks, strip piecing, and appliqué to interpret the feelings of movement and growth. Diagonal pattern placement and the spiral forms reinforce the theme. The piece measures 50 square inches and took about 10 weeks to complete.

Quilts~From Colonial to Contemporary

Helen Giddens's Rattle Family (45 × 60 inches) was inspired by snake rattles. The Texas quilter uses scraps for her pieced abstractions of Southwestern inspiration. The printed cloth is used like brushstrokes against the black ground, and the composition is full of movement, swirling around the somewhat sinister shapes of the "rattles" to produce a visually powerful piece.

Quilts~From Colonial to Contemporary

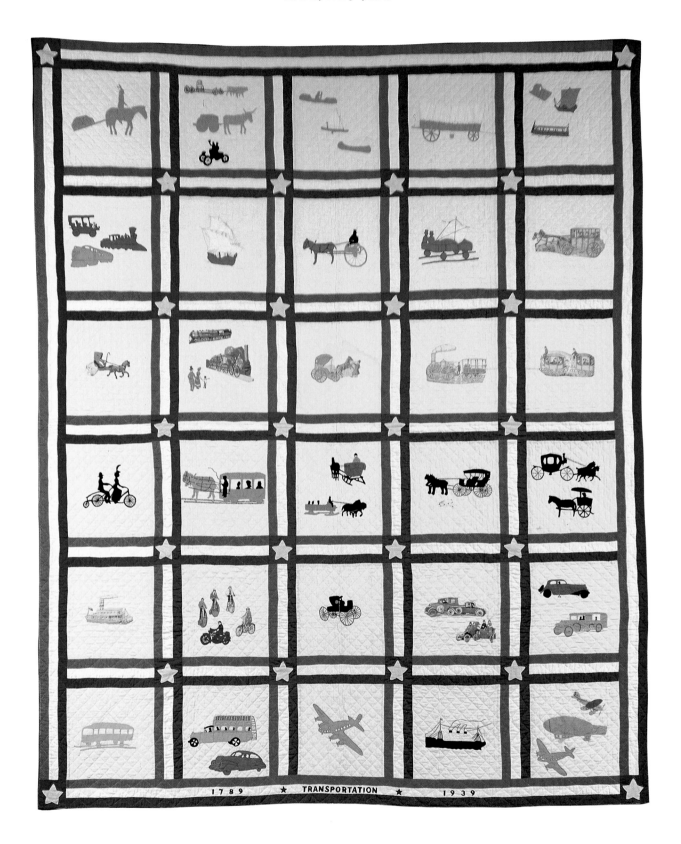

Contemporary Quilts

Popular among contemporary quilters is the "cause" or fund-raising quilt, designed to promote and financially aid anything from the Equal Rights Amendment to the local historical society. These are group quilts. Individuals contribute squares and help quilt the finished top—an activity reminiscent of earlier group quilting efforts. The quilt is then exhibited, raffled, or auctioned to raise funds.

Some group quilts feature pictorial appliqué interpretations of local history and buildings; others have environmental themes. Easily the largest, and among the most moving of these group quilts, is the AIDS Memorial

Quilt, shown in Washington, D.C., in 1989. It is a huge aggregate of 3 × 6-foot quilt panels, each made to honor a person who died from the disease. The quilt weighs 16 tons and could cover 14 acres.

Making a "cause" quilt is an ideal way for like-minded quilters to enjoy the social aspects of quilting while working for a cause.

Left: *The name* Transportation *may sound unimaginative, but great effort was lavished on this theme quilt, and the end product is unique and interesting. Above: AIDS NAMES was a recent and very poignant "cause" quilt that was created through an organized effort of the NAMES Project. It attempted to draw attention to the plight of the victims of AIDS.*

Quilts—From Colonial to Contemporary

This shows a section of the mammoth AIDS Quilt as it was displayed on the Capitol Mall in Washington, D.C., in 1989. Composed of individual quilts commemorating those who had died of AIDS to that date, the NAMES Project Foundation's AIDS Memorial Quilt is still being worked on today.

Quilts~From Colonial to Contemporary